To my [illegible]

BENEATH THE MOJAVE DESERT MOON

I hope you enjoy this book as much as I did writing it. I wish you all the best and hope you continue with your poetry as well. Take care.

POEMS

[illegible signature]

BENEATH THE MOJAVE DESERT MOON

by

Jason David Markiewitz

ISBN 0-9747259-0-0

Printed in the U.S.A. by
Morris Publishing
3212 East Highway 30
Kearney, NE 68847
1-800-650-7888

THIS BOOK IS DEDICATED TO:

My love, my best friend, my confidant, my inspiration and my strength, Diana
My grandparents, Louis and Nauwausau Markiewitz
My parents, David and Cheryl
My siblings, Kristi and Jonathan
My spirit's home, Tehachapi.
Agnes Harlow- whose memory lives on in us all
And Mark, Cindy, Linda, Carl, Kay, Grand-Al and Gram-Bea
And to all who have helped me put my words on paper, including:

--Tehachapi School System--
Mrs. Cleta Belt
Mr. Bill Richards
Ms. Barbara Teague

And, the CSU Fresno English Dept

CONTENTS

ACKNOWLEDGEMENTS

The Following Poems Have Been Included In These Works:

"A Golfer's Perception." In Dawn's Shadow: The International Library of Poetry. Watermark Press, 2001.

"A Golfer's Perception." Voices from the River Road. River Road Press, 2002.

"Meet Me in the Valley." Voices from the River Road. River Road Press, 2002*

"Sunshine." Passages in Time. JMW Publishing, 2001.

* 2nd Place Winning Poem in the "Poet's Voices" April 2001 National Competition

PREFACE

For the better part of ten years I have been putting my thoughts down on paper in various forms of poetic verse. Some of my earliest poems were written on notes I sent my wife when we were just in high school and those, too, are represented herein. Growing up in a small town, like Tehachapi, has given me a unique perspective on life and has provided me with a multitude of images to fuel my poetry. From the quiet nights in Golden Hills to the cacophonous rumblings of the freight trains passing through to the wildlife, both migratory and indigenous, which live in the mountains surrounding our town, Tehachapi is a little slice of heaven. It gives me great pride to say that I was born in Tehachapi, attended Wells and Golden Hills Elementary Schools, Jacobsen Junior High and Tehachapi High School. I am likewise proud to say that I have lived in Fresno, CA; Washington D.C.; San Angelo, TX; Kunsan City, Republic of Korea; Naples, Italy and California City, CA; and to me, there is still no finer place on earth than right here in the Tehachapi Mountains/Mojave Desert. With my father's parents living in Mojave, I have spent quite a many Sunday afternoon down there watching the ballgame with Grandpa and stuffing myself to the brim with Grandma's famous waffles. Memories like these are ones I will keep forever.

For me, poetry is a literary expression of mental images that need a voice to be heard, and have found that poetry is the most honest form of expression in the world. It is able to transcend time and place; it invigorates the senses and challenges the mind; it initiates thought and spurs creativity. It is my favorite form of expression and one that I am proud to share with everyone. It is unfortunate how in today's environment, poetic expression is a bad sale, a risky proposition and an endeavor the public, on the whole, seems not to appreciate. There is so much poetry in our everyday lives, from the earliest waking moment through the moon-cast shadows in the Mojave Desert nights, and all of it just beckons to be grasped. It is my hope that it *will* be grasped and that once again poetry receives the appreciation it once held the world over.

This collection of poems is designed to take the reader on a journey through life and love in a small community where you can still see the stars, where women are still treated with respect and where you can still enjoy the great outdoors without driving for hundreds of miles to get there. I hope you enjoy "Beneath the Mojave Desert Moon" as much as I enjoyed writing it.

JDM

OLD TOWN ROAD, TEHACHAPI

LIFE

Beyond the Turf

Through alabaster skies and cotton fog
O'er mountains purple and green
Cross brooks and creeks and meadows calm
Where cedar trees are queen

Under gray-white wind-swept clouds
'Round wind machines and trains
Beyond the turf and apple farms
In modest autumn rains

On breezes made from sapling oak
Above whirlwinds and dust
On occasion braving morning frost
To travel where they must

They crisscross through Tehachapi
En route to warmer zones
Leaving 'til the springtime chill will
Bring the turkey vultures home

Meet Me in the Valley

Meet me in the valley
Between the sagebrush and the pines
I'll sit up on a granite ledge
And feign to give no mind

I'll watch you, in my orange vest,
While you graze on live oak trees
I'll even speak without my tongue
To put your soul at ease

I'll keep myself upwind of you
So not to spoil your day
And promise not to take a step
That might be in your way

I'll stay here silent, on my rock
And watch the sun arise
To paint the ridge you're standing on
With solar compromise

But as the rays reflect your tines
You'd best be on your way
For if a buck, you prove to be
This could be your last day

The Morning Tryst

What consequence has brought you
From your bed across the frost?
You've stopped here on your morning tryst
Does your harem know you're lost?

I beseech you reconsider, now,
As your path is bleak with doom
For a score of hunters'll want your
Head atop their living room.

Look now! The puddle in my tracks
Does shake from trucks and foot
And whether they come driving by
Or ride a dapple's booted hoof

They'll see you. Then they'll wield rifles,
Then take aim and fire close at hand.
They'll wince a moment as the sound
Echoes 'cross the silent land

I feel them coming, ever more.
O, deer, they've got you in their lights
If you don't move now, you'll only
Be a second in their sights.

Go now, run fast, I've seen it all
What makes you freeze like so?
I tried to warn you, tragic buck,
You came to me for help,
And as venison you go.

My Golden Hills

I love my home, my Golden Hills
where stars shine through the night.
And I can hold my love, Diana,
beneath the deep silver moonlight

A place where if you stop and stand
and cast your cares away
You just might come to realize
there is no finer place

Just big enough to self suffice
and be all that we need
But small enough to be our home
devoid of "city" greed

The oak trees drop their acorns
on the cars and on the homes
And you will see the white surprise
as the winter snowfall comes

The spring is cool, bringing rain
to gardens, crops and creeks
And summer's mild humidity
makes this a place to seek

Autumn comes with changing leaves,
deciduous ones fall
And evergreens keep plugging on
to tempt the snowflake's fall

I love my home, my Golden Hills
where stars shine brilliant white
And I could hold my truest love
in sanctity all night.

Rhythm of the Wind

I was born in that old hospital.
So much has changed since then.
It's almost like a different song
floats on the rhythm of the wind.

Tehachapi was so much different
from the way it looks today.
I guess they call it progress, but
I sure did like the other way.

I've seen our golf course turn to weeds,
the very one I used to play.
I've seen the creep toward Golden Hills—
we used to be so far away.

Heck, we didn't have a Taco Bell,
Mickey D's or Burger King.
But we used to have the Warrior's Den
and Burger Spot was quite *the thing*!

There was no Albertson's on Tucker Road
and no Save Mart for your goods.
Because we used to shop at Town & Country
and get our meat from Valley Foods.

We didn't have Blockbuster Video,
or really any movie rental store.
There was no K-Mart Pharmacy,
but we did have Gong's Drugstore.

There was California Republic Bank
and KTPI was local still.
The post office was on Green Street,
not way down in Capital Hills.

And, what's with all the stoplights?
They're poppin' up in stacks.
We used to only have that one
before the Green St. Railroad Tracks.

There are some shops that I recall
that have lasted through the years.
And I hope they keep on trudging on
through these modernizing years.

Like Jim the Barber's Barber Shop
and Southern Shooter Supply.
There's still a Mountain Crossing
even though Mountain Lanes went dry.

We used to have Zond, then they left town,
and Enron moved right in.
Then they went Chapter eleven, and
we've got a name change yet again.

We're on the map for a new high school
to show what our progress's done.
But, how soon 'til the metal detectors'll
be searching for a hidden gun?

You can see it already around the town,
look how the children dress.
An influence of gangs and city life.
Another price of our progress.

As I get older and look back on
our town as it was then,
The more I wish I had the power
to change the rhythm of the wind.

The Rainbow

A band of colors span
the sky from sea to
shining sea;
A symbol of peace
an end to the storm
a declaration of
tranquility.

The Old Train Station

The ceiling's about to cave in
under the weight of all the snow.
The walls stand up in concrete stubbornness,
even though some've warped some time ago
yet stand rigid in their place. They stand as silent
guardians of what was in yesteryear.
Lasting every day, by tempting fate,
in hopes of preservation but with demolition's fear.
It clings to old Tehachapi with honor and grace,
though closed for quite some time.
And still the walls shake fiercely from
the Santa Fe and Southern Pacific lines.

As travelers stop at the oldest of our two
stop lights, and if their journey turns them north,
one constant in the universe they'll find is the
backed up cars as train then train go forth
to destinations all across the state.
but don't stop in our town anymore.
And year by year our old train station'll
send one more shingle cascading to the floor.

Tehachapi

A place where you can build a garden
Beneath a golden noon
A place where you can hold your sweetheart
Beneath a silver moon
A place where you can lose your identity
Beneath a clear blue sky
A place where you can find your happiness
Beneath a starry night
A place where you can leave your sins
Above God's very ground
A place where you can hear a thought
Betwixt the silent sounds
A place where you can spend a dime
And get a nickel's change
A place where you can live serene
On a mountain bordered range
A place where you can drive for hours
And end up right next door
A place where you can stop the clock
And time is never more
A place where you can hide from life
Between the apple trees
A place where you can raise your children
In safe communities
A place where you'll find timeless love
Where simplicity is king

A place where you can propose without
A thousand dollar ring
A place where you can build a fire
Inside from April rains
A place where you can hear the sounds
Of many distant trains
A place where you can make the rules
And live a ripened life
The place where I was fortunate
To meet my loving wife.

MEADOWBROOK PARK IN GOLDEN HILLS
SENIOR LEAGUE FIELD

Opening Day

What curse was cast to put me here
My breath shows frozen steam
My fingers blue, numb and stinging
Still I kick the rubber clean.

My ears are pounding, begging to
Be placed betwixt the heat
My eyes so cold, they tear with ice
The sign he must repeat.

Nodding affirmation sends a chill
Throughout my neck and spine
And I can only hope this full count pitch
Will hold it's truest line.

A frozen blow on colder hands
Won't warm them, not a bit
But still I blow, and check the runner
Then hurl toward the mitt.

The ball's release tears cross my finger
Tips as though an Indian burn
Speeding toward the plate in desperation
Of this batter's final turn.

The batter swings the bat around
And grits his teeth with might
But as the ump calls out strike three
The home team cheers alright.

And so the Angels beat the Cubs
On this traditionally freezing day
And the Tehachapi Valley Little League
Is officially underway.

Let's Run Through the Forest

Let's run through the forest, through
the oaks, the pines, the cedars standing
watch on the lakes, the brush, and around the
squirrels running 'round with acorns in their hands
in nature's desperation for the
winter food supply.

Let's run through the forest, through
the ivy, the live oak, the deer and cattle
grazing on the grasses beneath the canopy of leaves
and listen quietly as rutting bucks do battle
for the victor is awarded all
the harem's fondest eye.

Let's run through the forest, over
branches, moss and logs, around the mounds
from the gopher's self constructed home and halt
a moment, embracing the breeze and hearing the sounds
of nature's orchestra as they
play for you and me.

Let's run through the forest, over
hills and valleys, through the trees, to the edge
of the world, where no one has ever gone, where you and I
can look upon the land from on this ledge
and watch the soaring hawk glide
in complete serenity.

The Glen

Golden rays of light pierce through
the canopy and bless the ground,
They ride on heavy morning fog
marking paths to earth that Heaven found.
And split the trees as they traverse
the sky and clouds in warmth and light,
And signify through golden columns
an ending to the blackened night
and beginning of the day.

And as the chill escapes the glen
and life's awakened yet again,
The flowers bloom, the hustle goes
to feeding bucks and wary does.
And leaves begin to perk with life
as fog burns off in sacrifice,
For what once hid from dreary fog
stretches calmly on a warming log
to begin another day.

Beneath the Falling Snow

I looked out of my window
on one snowy afternoon
And watched the snowflakes glitter
painting everything in white

I went outside to stand alone
and feel the falling flakes
As one by one they floated by
illuminate and bright

My arms were covered fully
as was I, head to toe
With arms outstretched, poised statuesque
I lay down on the lawn

And refused to move an inch
as the snow kept falling
Painting me, enveloping me
'till I was covered white—and gone

Horsethief Number Three

Horsethief, par five, number three
A bending, lake-lined scene
From high atop the blue tee box
You can almost spy the green

A shining lake, a slicer's grave
In whose waters fish may come
Guards the fairway's right-hand side
From tee to flagstick's home

The willows drape a soft lament
As many golfers try
To drive a ball and cut the corner
But ultimately die

This treacherous monstrosity
Breathes fire from its core
And lurks in silence, waiting for
The next knock on its door

However tough, it can be tamed,
I've done it time and time again
But more than not you'll se the scores
Reflecting eight to ten

So, here's a tip, a pass-on log
From those who've gone before
If you hit an iron off the tee,
You may just get a four

The Miner
(For Grandpa)

The miner smokes a stogy
And sits back to relax
Alongside ore and dynamite
Away from phones and fax

He's taken tons of rock
From the bosom of the earth
And shipped it 'cross the desert
To be rewarded on its worth

And for ten times seven years
The miner's built his days
In Tonopah, Nevada mines
And in Mojave Desert clay

Now the miner's years are
Eighty-nine and change
And still he takes his satchel
To the Sierra Nevada Range

Because it does him well to get
Away from cities, phones, and fax
To a place where he can find some shade
And smoke a stogy and relax

LOUIS R. MARKIEWITZ

The Thief

Growing up in such a
town as this—
Where everyone knows
everyone—
Or at least, everyone
knows my family.
I seem to know most people,
and most people seem to know me.
Last night I saw a young man,
with whom I attended high school,
steal a shopping cart from K-Mart.
Shakespeare described this
individual in "Troilus and Cressida"
in the second act by saying,
"Thou hast no more brain than
I have in my elbows."
From my vantage point
I am hardly in a place to disagree.

Witness to a Suicide

The old man watched.
The warrior approached.
The lie was fair and true.

The trees gave way.
The wind held its breath.
And the sky turned gray to blue.

The warrior wielded his
Weapon and swung
For all his might.

The ball flew true.
Then half-way there,
Started banking to the right.

"What have you done?"
He called aloud.
And cursed the wretched swing.

And the old man watched,
As the lake engulfed it,
And he never said a thing.

Our First Home

The house next door isn't
That far away, separated
By the wall that encloses
Our backyard and lets
The birds build their nests
In our leafless tree.
Our first tree.
The patio isn't that small
For base housing, covered
By a lattice-work awning
Under-which we barbecue
And reminisce in the
Breezy Mojave nights.
Our first Desert nights.

The garage isn't that
Small, wall to wall with
Boxes and boxes and
Trophies and tennis rackets
That someday may be
Used for our car.
Our first car.
Our house isn't that
Small, in fact it's quite
Large for what most couples
Our age are living in.
Three beds, Two baths
In our new home.
Our first home.

The Drive
(Horsethief Number Twelve)

Standing atop the mountain, the
warrior fears no evil. His
weapon is forged with the finest
precision and crafted specifically
for this moment.

He stares into the abyss and
between towering oaks and
rolling hills spies his target.
It looms, cloaked by the shadows
of its guardians as they dare him
to enter their clutches.

He swings, carefully but
furiously and the
fairway waits patiently.

The trees extend their
clutches as far as can be with
the hopes of an interception.
The blade swings true, the guardians
retreat and the sun shines
its approval on the day.

A Golfer's Perception

Small circles, flattened tips of
Sunlight rays that penetrated
Through the canopy of
Oaks and pines
Onto the grass
Left a stationary
Image of a heavenly
Disco ball amidst
The shadows.
The six a. m. haze
Rode the beams
From sky to green
And painted their paths
With intangible strokes.
The solitary red flag
Stood proud and tall
As the newly risen sun
Blessed its very existence.

The Water Hazard
(Horsethief Number Three: Part II)

As a crocodile lurking from
beneath an unsuspecting fog
the danger awaits him.

It's not the typical enemy,
not stern or bold or brask,
but a death both quiet and grim.

It neither begs nor pleads
for certain fate, though
death is never far away.

And, at its base, it keeps
the hundred dozen
trophies on display.

The Mojave Desert Cactus
(AKA The Joshua Tree)

I am not a saguaro,
Though I am a cactus family friend,
I don't live in the typical desert,
But I love High Desert wind.
I have a unique design that's all my own,
And no other'll take my place.
I have been immortalized in desert art,
And have been slandered to my face.
I've had Desert links built all around me
As symbols of the land,
I've been peppered by golfers' errant shots
From tee to greenside sand.
Some people see me as an eyesore,
Others see a wise old man,
And some write poems of the desert
Through a miner's grandson's hands.
I had a choice of where to live
And thought for many moons,
Of just the perfect place to hear
A lonesome cowboy's tune.
The Saguaro went out Texas way
And I had sights on Mexico...
Though, I was certain that Mojave
was the finest place to go.
I've had quite a perfect life
And I still enjoy the wind.
So if you make your home out here,
I'll welcome you back in.

The Sun Beats Down Upon Us

The morning chill throws us all off
as the nights are cold and still.
Then the sun winks at the desert
and starts warming up the hills.
The breathtaking dawn is full of color
as the sun starts staring down,
And by mid-morning everyone
is in short-sleeves all over town.
By noon the sun beats down upon us
and the wind begins to blow
And by four o'clock it's one-o-five
above with five or ten to go.
At eight comes one last parting shot
and adios to one more day,
As the colors spring to life again
around a final golden ray.
As the wind dies down, the cool
Mojave nights grow deathly still.
And the Joshua trees leave silver
moon-cast shadows on the hills.

Remembering John

You wore a different uniform
and wore the number four.
We had just gotten to know each
other two or three years before.

You were pretty handy with a bat
and it was because of this we bet.
I bet I'd strike you out *this* year
'cause I hadn't done it yet.

In typical fashion we sparred back
and forth and finally agreed.
But the bet never came to fruition
as you died within the week.

I can't say I knew you all that well,
just on the diamond, I would guess..
And as far as "nice guys" were concerned,
All else seemed second best.

That next season we remembered #4.
My uniform was Chicago blue,
And the entire little league wore
patches in remembrance of you.

They emblazoned all our uniforms
and the umpires wore them too.
And after all these years, I still have
mine, in remembrance of you.

T
JOHN MENDEZ
1976
4
1989
ALL·STAR

Lurch

Playing basketball is just a hobby,
though friends of mine played well.
I would sometimes play some 1 on 1
to prove I still shot air balls well.

Every now and then I'd hit the court
with Ton and Lurch and Mark,
And play some vibrant 2 on 2 at
the school on Madre and Park.

The nets were lower, some 8 feet high
even I could *almost* dunk from there.
But Lurch was nearly six foot six
and that was not including hair.

We'd run up and down and cross the court
and sometimes make a shot.
And if we ever made two in a row
that meant someone just got hot.

And every so often, we'd get Lurch the ball
and sprint down the court to slam.
He'd run sort of clumsy, in his belt-less jeans
like a big basketball playing ham.

He'd get to the hoop and leap straight up
sending his hands up to the sky.
And as he went up….his pants went down
below his butt….down to the thigh.

We figured it would happen—since he had no butt
and his belt-less jeans were big.
We hadn't seen anything quite so funny
since Holly came to school in a wig.

After the dunk, ol' Lurch came down
and pulled his blue jeans high.
But, none of us had quite recovered
from the scene before our eyes.

He laughed a bit, his trademark laugh,
and gave his jeans a tug.
Then he grabbed the ball and tossed it in
with a goofy smile across his mug.

It's a scene we all remember
and will most likely keep in mind.
Not nearly as funny as the "Panda" joke
but quite a yarn from years behind.

The Bug

It was rusted and tarnished
and sore on the eyes.
It had no windshield, no doors
And no wheels on its sides.
It was small and compact
and always on the move.
It was a senior class icon
and a graduate's groove.
It would sit by the gym
or up on the grass.
It's been on the gym roof
but that didn't last.
It's been taken to pep rallies
and spray painted as well.
It's a THS legend
in a rusted out shell.

Our Small Mother Lode

Wind machines put us on the map.
They line the ridges of the hills
In a panoramic scene, some spinning
In the breeze, while others sit still.
They live in colonies of tens and hundreds
And can be watched all day from the road.
They used to be weird and seemed out
Of place, now they're our small mother lode.
There are short ones and tall ones and
Eggbeaters that decorate the sky;
Spinning hypnotically in concert
As travelers drive speedily by.
After all, they've become part of this town
And their praises are sung like a song.
What once was an eyesore is now beneficial
And, in the wind, we let them play along.

The Twentieth Freight Train

Walls shake,
Windows rattle,
People yell from two feet away.
Cars line up,
Drivers sit patiently,
It's the twentieth freight train today.

Spring

Gentle breezes whistle through the
cedars like an orchestra of flutes.
Through Stallion Springs and Golden Hills,
in Alpine Forest and the Piutes.

They bring with them 'bout every year
a cacophony of storms and rains,
where black clouds mix with thunder and
travel 'cross the sky as ghostly trains.

Their wheels send sparks of lightning through
the night in a magnificent display,
A web of electricity, and a
spectacle of light before the dawning day.

And, with that day comes harmony
as the conductor drops his hand
in one last haunting downbeat
for one last measure from the band.

The rains are now more of a gentle mist
as the night storm's ferocity's at peace,
and the flowers whose roots once hungered
now drink and eat a new life's lease.

They say April showers bring May flowers,
and, for the most part this is true.
But, sometime snow still falls in March
and May flowers bloom in June.

But when the flowers *do* bloom
it's a magnificent sight to see.
And it's a telltale painting of yellows
and oranges that Spring's in Tehachapi.

Stoney
(Based Upon Grandpa's Childhood Tale)

Stoney walked slowly,
Hunched forward as he trod
His knapsack thrown
O'er his shoulder, filled with sod.

The children called him names
And laughed when he went by
And Stoney gave them
All a look, from his solitary eye.

He owned a car, a Model-A,
Left in the yard to rust
That hasn't moved from ten
Years past, when he was told he must
Repair it on his own.

The townspeople smirked and
Laughed, and left him to his chores,
Inventing stories about his past,
Some ridiculous abstract lore.

And Stoney walked, from home
To town and home again,
Along the road and by
The school in sunshine, snow or rain.

And always had his faithful
Knapsack slung across his back
With a multitude of gardening
Things to place into his shack.

But no one ever witnessed
Stoney load or empty his bag
And the adults used this strange
Secrecy to pull a disciplinary gag.

And as their children misbehaved,
Instead of goin' out back
To cut a switch, they simply said:
"You're goin' in Stoney's sack."

The children, frightened white,
And scared of what he'd do
Behaved like young philosophers
And how diplomats would too.

They showed new respect for Stoney,
At least to him that's how it looked
And all the parents knew from then,
Their children had been hooked.

They stopped the lies, the stories,
And quit acting like a child
For Stoney, though a hermit
Cured their children from the wild.

Now the children call him “Sir”
And hush when he walks by
To let him go about his way
-- He and his solitary eye.

The Cowboy

The prairie dust is blowing
and his saddle is creaking
under his old chaps and jeans

While he pushes the cattle
through Indian battles
to wherever the money sings

His job and his life
take him far from his wife
but he can always hear her love song

And to him it's a wonder
her love's so deep under
to make her hang on for so long

His end is in sight
just one day and one night
then he'll tell her in person he loves her

But what she never knew
he was killed by a Sioux
and the cowboy rests alone in the thunder

The Last Fight Song

I see him standing down there
I know he'll turn around
I see we're patiently waiting
Scarcely making half a sound

Applause and screams erupt
As fans leap from seats and cheer
The Warriors score, we've won again
The title's ours for one more year

The referee's arms go vertical
And Wally turns around
I press the metal mouthpiece tight
For one more glorious sound

It's "Sons of Westwood," yet again
The down-beat strikes, we play,
For everything we're worth and more
In this, my last home game.

My trumpet's warm, the song is done,
The field is clear and cold
I put away my music, and my
Horn of black and gold.

LOVE

The Meadow Dancer

I saw you walking through a
meadow on one Sunday afternoon,
I watched you from a distance
as you danced and skipped. It was June

But something like November in the air,
Your sundress twirling, spinning
round, beneath those gorgeous locks
of auburn hair

You danced so light across the meadow
pirouetting round and round and round,
That your ankles brushed across the tips of the petals
of the flowers as you floated ‘cross the ground

I watched you find your way across
the purple dance floor to a stream.
A babbling brook, a running creek
and you, my perfect dream

I watched you skip a stone across
the water, then rest upon a rock.
Your sun dress, smile and golden eyes
would place a God in shock

I saw you dance back toward the
center of the meadow, stop and fall
collapsing on those purple flowers,
Beneath the wind and raven’s call

I laid myself beside you, wrapped my
arms around your waist, and sighed
I told you all the ways I love you,
Then I kissed your lips and cried.

If the Trees Could Talk

If the trees could talk,
What would they say?
Since they always see us walk by.
Would they say we're a couple?
Would they say we're in love?
Or would they just simply say hi?

Crystal Raindrop Blessings

We lay down on the mattress
made of grass and stared into
the blanket made of stars above.

We felt the breeze caress the blades
and rustle the leaves of the trees
who eavesdropped on our talks of love.

They listened as we told each
other how we felt, how we loved,
Then the sky rained silent tears.

It was the Heavens sending a
billion crystal raindrop blessings
for a thousand happy years.

TEHACHAPI MOUNTAINS SOUTH OF BACKES ROAD

The Chill of the Air

The chill of the air,
The nip of the night,
The old man moves
by candlelight.
Winding through trees,
And guarding the moon,
As distant coyotes
howl outlawed tunes.
The wind plays her flute,
The sun's down 'til dawn,
And through the
mist and the cold
he moves on.

Smack in the Middle of Dodger Country

Some people cheered in fifty-four,
Some people may still be.
Some people cried in eighty-nine,
Some people just like me.
Some saw hope in ninety-three,
And again in ninety-seven.
But, we cried again in ’02
As their loss came down from heaven.
Next year will be fifty years
Since the Giants won it all,
And I’ll be bleeding black and orange
‘Til ‘04’s summer turns to fall.

Here, smack in the middle of Dodger country
No one cares about my plight,
Since their team won in eight-eight
And Gibson’s homer stole the night.
But neither Gibson, Clark nor Sax
Are playing ball these days.
So, I guess it’s up to Barry Bonds
To bring some light into the haze.

Here’s to the shot heard ‘round the world
And to next year’s Giants team,
In hope they’ll bring a ring and seal
A long lost San Francisco dream.

Only 20mm Long

Was I running?
Maybe jogging?
What was it affecting my heart?
What made me feel such excitement?
And why was I smiling from ear to ear?
No P.T.
No 5K.
Just the sight of my wife with gel on her belly
and the doctor's wand pressed to her stomach.

And that!

That little image on the screen,
Measured from rump to crown.

Our baby.

Our first baby.

Only 20mm long.

She Slept on my Shoulder

A year ago I tore every
ligament in my right
shoulder. The pain was
amazing. Intense.
Excruciatingly sharp.
I slept sitting in a
Lazy Boy recliner for
almost a month.

Lying down was painful.
Standing up was painful.
Walking, breathing and
talking was painful.
And now, a year later,
I can smell her hair,
her warm breath on my
chest; the gorgeous jewel
who nursed me to health;

I gently kissed her forehead as
she slept on my shoulder.

She Lies Quietly

She lies quietly, sleeping,
Unaware of my presence
Though my caresses have
run across her body for hours.

I watch her sleeping,
Unwilling to lose sight of her
For even a minute though I
have to sleep sometime.

I kiss her, sleeping,
Unwaveringly professing the love
I offer so frequently and
feel so fortunate to receive.

A Better Me

I sometimes wonder how my life would be
If I were not with you
Where would I be, what would I
Be doing…and with whom?

Would I be a multi-millionaire?
A pauper or a clown?
Would I be a doctor or a Lumberjack
In a Humboldt County town?

Would I be a famous novelist?
A teacher of fine arts?
Or perhaps an L. A. counselor to
Mend some wounded hearts?

Would I be a better person than the
One I am today?
Would I be a known celebrity
On the silver screen or stage?

Would my parents be more proud of me
Than they always seem to be?
Would I ever love another half as much
As I love thee?

And when that question comes around
I know the theory's done
For your love makes my whole existence
The best of anyone

You are the angel who spreads her wings
And covers me in love,
The girl who backs me in my goals
My wonderful white dove

You instill in me the want to be
An impassioned, loving man
The way you love, the way you smile
As only heaven can

You are the perfect woman all the
Boys just dream to meet
And for your love and adoration
Life would be so very sweet

I know the only way in life
I'd ever be a better me
Is to always have you in my life
And let me cherish thee

Dance

It fills her life with passion
It liberates her soul,
It makes her dreams reality
And completes a lifelong goal.

It wakes her in the morning
It keeps her out all night,
It’s like a met amphetamine
Floating on the neon lights.

It gives her bold new challenges
It tests her skills each time,
It leads her round from club to club
With Tequila, salt, and lime.

It soaks her in a lathered sweat
It varies step and beat,
From tap to Mexican folklorico
To a clogger’s dancin’ feet.

It’s in her blood, she can’t deny
It echoes in her ears.
And if she’d live a century more,
She’d dance all hundred years.

Wounds of War

She wears a
band-aid on
her finger
and a claw
to keep her
hair out of
the meatloaf.
Her hands show
wounds of war
in the kitchen
with various
appliances,
utensils and
glass.
The least I
could do was
set the table.

The Moon Shone Bright

The moon shone bright
in the valley tonight
as we went for a walk in the park

You held my hand tight
as we walked in moonlight
and your eyes gleamed like stars in the dark

Your dress off the shoulder
was calling “Come hold her”
as I put my arms ‘round you we kissed

When my kiss hit your neck
you threw your head back
and I realized how much I’d missed

We kept up for hours
then I gave you three flowers
and told you my love was true

Then you took my hand
and said “You’re my man”
and that you loved this poor fellow, too.

When We Were Just Kids

Many years ago when
we were just kids and
love was a feeling
everyone seemed to have
at least twice a week,
I only truly had once.

You.

When I Close My Eyes

When I close my eyes
I see your smile.
When I go off to dream
I see us for a while.

I see the gleam in your eyes,
And the spark in your charm,
And the loving way you squeeze
When you hang onto my arm.

All of these things
I hope will come true,
And you will
Forever be mine

So let's take our love
And let's let it grow,
And take it one
Step at a time

I Hopelessly Hope

From when the sun comes up
Until it sets in the night
You're the beat of my heart
And the star in my eye
And I hopelessly hope
We never say Good Bye

Shadows on the Moon

The desert storm has cleared,
and the wind is just a breeze.
I have no doubt that I could hear
a kangaroo rat sneeze.

Across the yard, the neighbors
frolic in the swimming pool
as I stand on our bedroom deck
and hold my sweet high desert jewel.

We close our eyes and feel the wind
pass softly through our clothes,
And listen to the silence
as the night walks on its toes.

The stars flickered like disco lights
to an orchestrated tune,
And tiptoe across the Milky Way,
beyond the shadows on the moon.

I'd Harness the Moon

I'd harness the moon
I'd lasso a star
I'd fly 'round the world
To be where you are

I'd walk 'cross the Gobi
And climb up K2
I'd swim the Pacific
To be next to you

The Vision

Have you ever seen a woman who
could stop the hands of time?
Who had a face, so pure and sweet,
'Twas like a vintage wine.
In whose eyes you lost your train of thought,
A blanking of your mind.
Whose voice so soft and beautiful,
T'would make your soul unwind.
Whose auburn hair, flowed and
Curled, extended toward her waist.
With lips so soft, voluptuous,
You yearned each day to taste.
And a body so seductive, with
The perfect form and size
That you would give your final breath
And risk your own demise
To have her on your arm forever?

I saw that woman some years ago,
And tripped and fell in love.
She remains the woman of my
Dreams, my light from up above.
And every day I love her more,
For that vision's now my wife
The girl who shares my every dream
And complements my life.
So if you need to see a woman who
Could stop the hands of time,
You needn't look much further
Than that gorgeous wife of mine.

Sitting by You on the Lawn

Sitting by you on the lawn by the court
Even though the weather is cold.
We're holding hands and babe we're together
And my heart burns warm and bold.

As I feel that our feelings keep getting stronger,
I think of you more and more.
I stare at your picture and re-read your letters
And wish you'd show up at my door.

The air could be twenty or thirty below
But with you always I'm warm.
And my love for you will last forever
Through any tempestuous storm.

Diana

Diana, with hair sandy brown,
With skin as soft as partridge down,
One look from her eyes
Makes me realize
No sweeter love I've ever known

Sunshine

You are the sunshine
In my every moment
And my silver lining
'Round clouds of gray
And skies of ash.
The light you give
My life and the
Meaning you give
My whole existence
Are treasures I
Will always strive to
Possess—yet be
Forever unable
To repay.

What You Do For Me

I buy you flowers and
Take you to dinner and
Help you with your
Homework

You always talk about
Me doing things and
The gifts of love
I present to you

What you don't know is
What you do for me.

I’ve Heard; I’ve Seen

I’ve heard our love
Pronounced in the wind.
I’ve heard our love
In strength will bend.
I’ve seen the reflection
Of us in the lake
I’ve seen what happens
When love’s not forsaken.
Every heartbeat that
Pounds through my soul
Reverberates gently
Like soft rock and roll.
Like the bloom of a flower
On a rain-speckled day
You’re the queen of my
Dreams, night and day.

I’ve heard our love
Rampaging down streams,
I’ve heard our love is
Dictating our dreams.
I’ve seen our love
Growing steadily better
I’ve seen it improving
With each new love letter.
I hope we can keep our
Love steady and strong
As year upon year we
Sing our love song.

I Live

You serve,

You volley,

You win,

You travel,

You learn,

You study,

You succeed,

You graduate,

You work,

You love,

You dance,

You live.

You smile,

I live.

One Kiss From You

One kiss from you
And I forget the world.
No matter where
No matter why
It sends a charge
Between us

Holding you close
To me makes me feel
Like a king.

With all your beauty
And radiant charm,
I love having
You in my life.

Sunset on Kaua'I
(Our Honeymoon)

Sunset on Kaua'I
Is a breathtaking event.
Romantic, enchanting,
Relaxing, as the sun
Ducks beneath Mother
Earth's wing.
When couples like us
Walk barefoot in the sand
With their shoes in
Their hands,
Sensing that feeling
Only the beach
Can provide.

Sometimes

Some-
times
Peoples' words,
Though in jest, are mistaken.
And humor
Can pierce
A heart
With the
Might
of a
Sword

JOSHUA TREE IN THE MOJAVE DESERT

Waffles and a Ballgame

Few things compare to
Sunday afternoons at Grandma's.
The aromas from the kitchen and
the sizzling of the sausages are
only overshadowed by the company.
It's a beautiful thing.
Waffles and a ballgame.
Golden Belgian waffles,
round…not square,
whipped cream and peanut butter
smothered under maple syrup.
On the TV it's the Angels, the Dodgers
or the Lakers…
and now the Diamondbacks,
or as Grandpa says, "the rattlesnakes."
It's a beautiful thing.
Waffles and a ballgame.
We sit at the small table for four
with the ballgame on in the background.
And, after seconds…and sometimes thirds,
Grandpa and I go watch the game…
and Diana and Grandma talk over coffee.
It's a beautiful thing.
Waffles and a ballgame.
Only overshadowed by the company.

The Watch

We put the cattle in the pasture
And tied the horses to the rail
Jim fixed up a small campfire
'Bout twenty paces from the trail

The rain's been light
Like a month long haze
Don't 'spect no one quite remembers
When we had a sunny day

The coffee's weak, the food is bad
Look's like "Cookie's" on the take
I ain't slept a wink in upteen days
It's like I've always been awake

Drips are falling off my wide felt brim
Lightning tears across the night
Frank's sittin' watch above the herd
You can see him up against the sky

I should be sleeping.
Frank's itchin' to be relieved
And it's purd'near time I ran along
So he can get some sleep

But if I know Frank, he'll mosey down
And grab some food and joe
And I 'spect he'll wake up in the morn'
Rip Roarin' and ready to go

But I sure as hell hope this rain quits soon
As we drive the herd to Dodge
In the meantime though I'll drink my joe
And go and take the watch.

His Southern Belle

The war kicked off in forty-one
and he was nearly thirty-five,
Two of his brothers were stationed at Pearl
and somehow both survived.

He chose the army in forty-two
though he didn't have to go,
And, finished his training in Missouri's
cold mid-western snow.

Before the army shipped him out
he went to Mobile for a spell,
And, while on relaxation time
met a lovely southern belle.

They saw each other only once
before he shipped out to the Med,
But visions of that afternoon
were engraved inside their heads.

For two years they wrote back and forth
as the war raged on and on,
And, though she dated other men
her true-love soldier-boy was gone.

He thought about her day and night
and she missed him all the time,
It was a poem whispered 'round the world
where the stanzas didn't rhyme.

When the war ended in forty-five
he found himself again on board
a troop ship; This time taking service-
men back home to friendly shores.

Once the ship pulled in he caught a train
then processed himself out.
Then headed straight back to Mobile
to get the girl he'd dreamt about.

Their letters kept them faithful
to each other while he fought,
And, beneath the Alabama sun
they agreed to tie the knot.

He was eighteen years her senior
and when they met she seemed so young,
But the bud he left in forty-two
had surely blossomed in the sun.

They wed in nineteen forty-five
and he took his bride out west,
From her antebellum southern home
to his Mojave Desert nest.

The trees she grew up with were gone,
the sage was tall; the air was dry;
She dearly loved her soldier boy
but that desert made her cry.

And, Mojave was a rowdy town
with saloons as far as she could see,
And, the only law around this place
mostly drank himself to sleep.

But, no matter how the first impression
made the tears flow from her eyes,
She stood beside her soldier boy
in a western wife's disguise.

As the years passed by she watched that town
from a distance nevertheless,
And even grew to call it home
though at first with some duress.

He always told her that he loved her
from the moment that they met.
It surely helped to ease the pain
and quell that last regret.

For fifty years they've lived there.
She made a Heaven from the hell.
'Cause she still loves her soldier boy,
and he sure loves his southern belle.

The Wind was Angry Today

The wind was angry today,
and was itching for a fight.
The clouds were gray and dark,
making noon like early night.
The trees leaned over anyhow,
since they grew in desert gusts.
And the sand flew 'round hysterically
to make a fog of desert dust.

The wind was angry today
and made the birds fly statuesque.
Even the Joshuas started to sway
as the storm grew more grotesque.
The darkened clouds began to cry,
then threw bolts against the ground.
And, the smell of ozone in the air
made it all seem right somehow.

Yes, the wind was angry today
and the desert felt its wrath.
From bird to hare to gopher snake
it touched all that crossed its path.
We sat in the bed of the pickup truck
and watched it all take place.
It was hell on earth mixed gently
with the purest Heaven's grace.

An Absence of Smog

An absence of smog is noticed
From the moment you arrive.
Breathing doesn’t make you cough
And there’s no burning in your eyes.
From daybreak on to evening’s call
The sky is blue and clear,
And red-tails fly against the breeze
For more than half the year.
The wind blows through the grasses
And the clouds are pearly white.
And as the evening brings the moon,
You can see the stars all night.
An absence of smog makes this all happen,
It’s what first made people move.
From in the valley to ‘round the loop,
And why Tehachapi’s so loved.

The Moment We Saw Her

The moment we saw her we knew she was perfect.
Her cute little nose, her light brown hair,
Brown eyes that radiated the evening sun,
And those cute little feet we could already hear
Going pitter-patter around the hardwood floor.
We wanted one. We thought about it for years.
We were stable and had a nice house.
It was time and we knew it.
We hadn't picked out a name, so on the way home
We selected a name that matched her personality.
Desdemona. She was regal.
Our little Desi.
She was our first.
And we love her so much.
She slept with us on our bed
for the first few months.
But then Desi had to make her place
In the world.
Our little Desi.
Our first puppy.
And we loved her
From the moment we saw her.

There's a Glow Around Her Face

If you've ever been married, you know what I mean.
There's a glow around her face,
her entire body,
her skin.
Slowly, she's outgrowing her clothes
The baby needs room to grow,
to develop,
to move.
A son.
A daughter.
It's still too early to tell.
Either way, it will be cared for,
cherished,
worshiped,
loved.
Every bit as much as its mother,
whose glow lights up my life.

The Fourth of July

The fourth of July.
Independence Day.
The country celebrates with fireworks,
and firecrackers,
some legal
and some not,
But all leave trails of gunpowder in the night.
As a kid in Tehachapi I'd watch from our house.
Sure, it was more than 10 miles away,
but we sat up on the pool wall
and enjoyed the spectacle over the trees.
As a teen I went to the park
and, sometimes,
watched them from the bed of a pickup truck.
Thirty minutes,
hundreds of blasts,
dozens of kisses,
one beautiful woman.

Alzheimer's Onset

Who's that girl?
She's awfully nice.
Do I know her?

That's Cheryl.

Oh. She seems nice.

She's your daughter.

And who's that?
I think I recognize her?
I think I've seen her before?
Do you know who that is?

That's your wife.

Oh. Yes, uh huh.

It's a detestable thing.
Alzheimer's.
To happen to a man so smart,
a medical doctor,
a man who has saved lives,
a musician,
a veteran,
a husband,
a father,
My mother's father.
a grandfather.
My grandfather.
I hope he's happy,
At peace with himself,
and having dreams
that are crystal clear.

Photographic Credits

“Joshua Moon”*	by: Cheryl J. Markiewitz	Cover, 69
“Old Town Road”	by: Jason D. Markiewitz	x
“Senior League Field”	by: Jason D. Markiewitz	15
“The Miner”*	by: Cheryl J. Markiewitz	23
“All Star Uniform”	by: Jason D. Markiewitz	33
“South of Backes Rd”	by: Jason D. Markiewitz	53
“Joshua Tree”	by: Jason D. Markiewitz	80
“Spying the Moon”*	by: Cheryl J. Markiewitz	Back

* Photograph used with permission of photographer

ABOUT THE AUTHOR

Jason David Markiewitz was born in Tehachapi, California in February of 1976 and lived there for 18 years. Following graduation from Tehachapi High School in 1994, he attended California State University-Fresno where he majored in Political Science and minored in Aerospace Science. During his time at CSUF, though engulfed in classes to support his major, he also spent many hours taking creative writing classes through the English Department. In May of 1998 he received his Bachelor of Arts degree in Political Science as well as a commission in the United States Air Force as a Second Lieutenant. Currently he is serving on active duty as a Captain with the USAF and stationed at Edwards Air Force Base in the southern California Mojave Desert.

Jason is also the owner of Rhythm Wind Games, a board game development company that is in production of a baseball-genre traditional family board game called "Safe at Home" due out in 2004.

Diana is the owner of Diana's Enchanted Aisle, a full-scale wedding coordination business, is professionally trained by the Association of Certified Professional Wedding Consultants, and is a member of the Bakersfield Bridal Association. She has successfully planned a number of weddings over the past two years and is in demand already for the spring of 2004.

ORDER FORM

Additional copies of this book are available by mail and ONLINE!

If ordering by mail:
Send check or money order (payable to: Jason David Markiewitz) to

BENEATH THE MOJAVE DESERT MOON
9849 KAREN AVE
CALIFORNIA CITY, CA 93505

Or, visit our listing on Amazon.com......

Or, visit your local bookseller, coffee shop or gift store.
(If they don't carry it...tell them they should!!!)

Be sure to visit www.highdesertwriter.com for periodic offers, discounts and information on upcoming works/events...

✂---

I WOULD LIKE TO ORDER THE FOLLOWING WORK: (Tax & Shipping Included*)

TITLE	QTY	PRICE EA.	TOTAL
BENEATH THE MOJAVE DESERT MOON	______	$14.05	____________

*Tax = 7.25%; Shipping based upon USPS Media Mail 2-3 lbs = $2.26
- Domestic Standard 3-7 day Shipping Only